THE ELEMENTAL WARRIORS

A BOOK OF GREEN THOUGHTS BY M. RAJARAM

THE ELEMENTAL WARRIORS

A BOOK OF GREEN THOUGHTS BY M RAJARAM

FOREWORD BY DR. APJ ABDUL KALAM

RUPA

First published in 2011 by
Rupa Publications India Pvt. Ltd.
7/16, Ansari Road, Daryaganj
New Delhi 110002

Sales centres:
Allahabad Bengaluru Chennai Hyderabad Jaipur Kathmandu Kolkata Mumbai

Second impression 2012

ISBN: 978-81-291-1743-4

10 9 8 7 6 5 4 3 2

Printed in India by
Nutech Photolithographers
B-240, Okhla Industrial Area, Phase - I
New Delhi 11020, India

TABLE OF CONTENTS

INTRODUCTION

With all this talk about global warming and climate change, we do tend to forget some of the more fundamental things we take for granted, like getting up in the morning and brushing our teeth with the tap running, enjoying that tetra pack of juice before throwing it away, playing on the computer, carefully saving the game on stand-by for later viewing, or perhaps being dropped to school or college in the car. We forget, like most adults, that running water is precious water wasted, getting rid of garbage from our house does not mean it disappears, a computer on stand-by for hours is not conserving energy, and petrol is not endless. We forget that tomorrow is another day, another time, another space. We forget that our planet Earth is a living, breathing entity like us. And we need to start thinking about it today.

This is not yet another wake-up-call-to-climate-change book, nor does it list out sordid details about the irreparable effects of global warming. I believe we have reached the point where we need to go beyond this mere panic mode we seem to be in that either leads to pessimism or indifference. We need to move ahead, we need optimism and hope, and as humans we do have an incredible capacity to move mountains with just that.

And so, we have 'The Elemental Warriors', Air, Water, Fire and Earth, who take us through this journey of hope. We have them teach us how we can, as individuals, do a lot more than we think. And we have their 365-day planner on simply practising one green thought a day. It's all we need to keep that tomorrow green and safe.

Dr. M. Rajaram

Dr. APJ Abdul Kalam
Former President of India

September 24, 2010

Foreword

The earth is heating up due to global warming. The globe is warming up due to undesirable practices of the people. As on 2007, the Carbon dioxide emission worldwide stood at roughly 30 billion tons or 30 Gigatons annually. This means that we are adding about 2 parts per million of Carbon dioxide every year. Such imbalances have been more significant since the industrial revolution. Analysis shows that the CO_2 concentration has risen from the pre-industrial figure of around 280 parts per million in 1750 to about 384 ppm in 2007.

The impact of global warming is already being felt across multiple environmental aspects and throughout the world. Meteorological data shows that there has been a significant upward trend in the average temperature in all the continents across the globe. In the past two centuries, the rise in temperature has been almost 1°C on land and more than 0.5°C in the oceans reflecting an overall rise of 0.8°C. In fact, since 1970, most of the regions and countries of the world have witnessed temperature rise of varying intensities.

Hence there is a need for sensitizing people on green practices. A book like "The Elemental warriors" by Dr Mr. Rajaram will surely come in handy to spread eco-awareness among the people, youth and students. The poems in Air, Fire, Water and Earth are commendable and disclose the imperative value of the natural elements.

The "Green thoughts" give "One Eco-Action a Day" that would keep global warming at bay. These thoughts for each day would be immensely valuable for the people, not only to reduce global warming but also to save time, energy and money.

This is a book to be in the hands of everyone, particularly the younger generation.

APJ Abdul Kalam

10, Rajaji Marg, New Delhi – 110 011, India
Email: apj@abdulkalam.com
www.abdulkalam.com

ACKNOWLEDGEMENTS

When this book took root in my mind, I didn't realise how daunting the process would turn out to be. I ended up spending years collecting material from various newspapers, magazines, CDs, films, books … the list is endless. And then it took months going over the material, deliberating over its contents and waiting for the book to finally take the shape it has today.

The book would have never seen the light of day without the unstinting cooperation of my well-wishers and friends. I thank Mr. S. Velliyangiri, Mrs. Anitha Krishnaswamy, Ms. Praveena Shivram, Mr. D. Varadarajan, Mr. C. S. Kalyanasundaram, Mr. P. Jayeraj and Mr. V. Rajagopal for their assistance. I would also like to thank Global Adjustments Services Pvt. Ltd. for their unstinting support and constructive suggestions.

And finally, I would also like to thank Rupa Publishers for standing by me and providing insightful guidance in the book projects I undertake.

Dr. M. Rajaram

PROLOGUE
BEFORE THE BEGINNING

Every creation comes with its challenges. Planet Earth is no different.

I think the best thing ever created on the Planet Earth is the apple. It is always best tasting when sitting on fluffy clouds. But well, every creation can never be fully experienced by everyone, all the time.

When I released the blue-green waters (because I liked the colours), I didn't realise the havoc it would end up causing. You can never know the full potential of every creation you create.

Now Air, that's quite something else. It just had to be mildly altered for the Planet Earth. Every creation can always be changed, anytime, anywhere.

Fire, for sure, was an accident. A clumsy dragon left loose. Every creation is partly made of such mistakes. Always.

And finally, Earth, the ground beneath your feet. Different from the Planet itself. Every creation is known only by its worth, not by its name.

My four Warriors come together in a fifth, Ether, because every creation is always a sum of many parts.

Not to forget the music! Every creation is best remembered in a tune. Try it.

They call me by many names, but mostly I like to be called 'The One'. Every creation, is finally, the choice you make. And the responsibility you then partake.

THE SONG OF AIR

From the swirling mists of matter
I rise forth within you
Taller than you or shorter
I am even in a drop of dew.

I call out to you every day
Sometimes softly sometimes piercingly
When lost, I could show you the way
If you can read me correctly.

I am the mighty and meek Air
Mighty because of my immense power
Meek because of my obvious lack of flair
And yet, I exist, like a strong, silent tower.

If you are wondering why now
Why this sudden gust of words
Then allow me to take a bow
Before picking up my swords.

For fight I will, no matter what
To save the purity of my clan
Pollution, dust, smog and the lot
Can very well live with man.

But I fear for you my friends
As I look into the near future
The darkness quickly descends
Hence I speak, will you listen to this creature?

My story begins a million years ago
When nothing was everything
And time, a friend, not a foe
That glides across the Eternal Ring.

Slowly we lived and breathed
Steadily we reigned supreme
Till one fine day the atoms seethed
And we knew, this was no dream.

It crackled with vigour and power
Right next to planet Mars
It was a veritable shower
Of a multitude of twinkling stars.

With a resounding clap of thunder
And the hopeful rumble of rain
We watched in awestruck wonder
The creation of Earth off a single grain.

How we rejoiced and sang and danced
To witness a miracle in front of our eyes
From one galaxy to another we pranced
Till the arrival of the One, so wise.

"Indeed, this is what we waited for"
"The perfect planet with the perfect core"
"Now don't ask me for more"
"Till you explore this planet's lore."

"To harbour and nurture peace"
"Earth comes with a special soil"
"Production of this will never cease"
"Till the clan of Air will always toil."

"But beware O mighty clan"
"For there will come a time"
"When the relentless pursuits of man"
"Will spread this planet with grime."

And so here I am, the First Warrior
Surveying the damage already done
I can hear the miscreants savagely jeer
As they loot the environment for fun.

$C0_2$ and Methane vie for attention
As poisonous gases beat Oxygen down
All of them float in vivid suspension
Of human disbelief, a collective noun.

I know, they are all a part of me
And I can't possibly ignore them
I accept the good, the bad, and the ugly
For they flourish out of my stem.

I saw you, O Human, when you began
Taking baby steps on this new Earth
I was (and remain) your biggest fan
You know not still, your own worth.

I saw you pull down the first tree
And ingeniously make your first wheel
I applauded your ability to see
Beyond the simple necessity of the next meal.

Rapidly you grew into what you are today
An ambitious, talented, wonderful achiever
I wondered what all the fuss was about anyway
Why did the One warn me, a believer?

Then I saw you quickly plummet
As you razed the environment
Faster than a speeding bullet
With a complete lack of emotion, or sentiment.

You forgot you were a part of it
And moved away, as though adrift
I was now choked in soul and spirit
And needed reinforcements to fix it.

The planet I knew so dearly
Was withering in front of me
My own clan was perishing slowly
I couldn't keep quiet, I couldn't just be.

To flush out all the dirt
I needed some solid support
To the Second Warrior I did blurt
The call for action at Justice Court.

THE SONG OF FIRE

Twisting, seething, glowering, burning
Leaping, fluttering, crackling, growling
Fire, the Second Warrior is now arriving
Beware! Your excuses I am not buying!

You think you can get away with this
Then let me tell you my story
Listen now, be careful not to miss
Even if it gets a bit too gory.

It's true I came to help and aid
Providing warmth, energy and light
Evolution was far from staid
And I tried to keep things in sight.

It was all very well then
As new places we discovered
Till we stepped into the dark den
And I saw in you, a shaky coward.

That very instance I decided
This man species is quite redundant
It's not so much what you did
But how you did and simply went.

With blinkers you marched ahead
Into the shimmering light of success
You cared not what you led
A riot of destruction, a royal mess.

Sure it's important to "develop"
To rise up, to reach new heights
But you also need to follow-up
Things left behind, like abandoned kites.

I saw how you dug deep
Into the essence of the planet
The seeds of desire you did reap
It was limitless, and you were set.

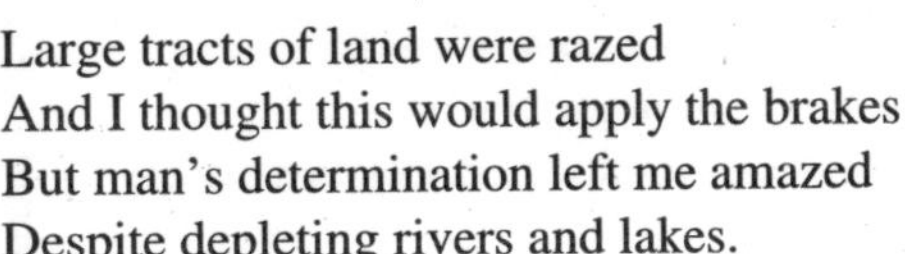

I saw the forests disappear
And all the buildings sprout
It became worse with each passing year
Yet, you never stopped in doubt.

Sure, you felt rightly safe and sound
Within the four walls of your house
It would have been all right all around
If you'd spared a thought for that leaf, or mouse.

So I took matters into my hand
And decided to really help man
Since he did destroy all his land
Why not speed things up when I can?

In a twinkling of an eye
Forest fires and volcanoes erupted
I did hear the combined outcry
But to me, it sounded only corrupted.

Large tracts of land were razed
And I thought this would apply the brakes
But man's determination left me amazed
Despite depleting rivers and lakes.

They devised more and more means
That pushed them further away
From nature and closer to their machines
It was one long night, with no sign of day.

Now, I am old and exhausted
All that rage and anger left me tired
Nothing I did really accosted
What man insatiably desired.

I went to the forest I had recently razed
And walked about assessing the damage
When I saw this little girl unfazed
By the incessant debris and garbage.

She was kneeling on the ground
Patting something I couldn't see
I had to softly walk around
And beheld the unexpected, believe me.

She was saving a lone sapling
That had somehow escaped the fire
I could even hear her sing
A tune that melted the ire.

Oh, I was ashamed, I was
My folly was my futile revenge
With my own behaviour I was cross
Who was I trying to avenge?

In that hot, barren land
She sat alone with her tree
Through her fingers the grains of sand
Settled beneath, protected and free.

I knew I had to help her
That's what I was made for
I was not meant to suffer
In the heat of my ignominy.

Fire is good, fire can be bad
They sure exist simultaneously
No point getting depressed or sad
Need a solution now, quickly.

And so I called out to the Third
The Warrior of regeneration
I sent the message through a bird (I know)
It was time for some fortification.

THE SONG OF WATER

I felt the soft splash of the pebble
And felt light in the heart
I see it sink below to the rubble
Into my distant memory cart.

For I still remember the time
When abundance didn't scare me
When synchronicity wasn't only in rhyme
When all I did was flow serenely.

The rains were in my command
And so were the pristine oceans
The glaciers and ice seldom demand
For more than nature's simple notions.

It was wonderful to feel the drop
Why not, I was the heavenly carrier
Of all things liquid, bottom to top
For I was Water, the third Warrior.

Soon the adventure began to nurture
This planet's self-sufficient well
It was a part of my inherent culture
To sustain and contain the swell.

I was delighted to be of service
As humanity continued to flourish
I was in a state of complete bliss
In my stupor, I was indeed foolish.

Lost in mankind's beatific smile
I lost my sense of balance
In man's endless pit of guile
It changed my rhythm, my cadence.

Please don't think I was cheated
Or that I am justifying my regret
We are all part of the One who created
No…I really, don't want to fret.

I am the one called Water
I only follow the course of flow
Where or how does not matter
As long as I continue to go.

In my defence, I wasn't prepared
For the onslaught to come
If I had known, I would have cared
Maybe even saved the planet some.

Ground water got infected first
That quickly left the wells dry
Irrigation systems were now cursed
And the rains started to bid goodbye.

I pushed myself harder to keep
Things from falling apart drastically
The challenge became a bit too steep
When even the oceans became sickly.

They were being pushed back for land
Which caused an ugly rebellion
There was nothing I could do to disband
I was out of balance and reason.

I tried to solve this alone
I am the life-giver, I know
But down to my very bone
I was tired, exhausted and very low.

I continued to flow humbly
There was nothing else to do
I witnessed the lack of respect fully
And all I did was to rue.

But one day I stopped to look
As a kangaroo lay dead
During the drought it mistook
The mirage shimmering ahead.

Misery and rage took over
My already imbalanced state
With no strong emotional armour
I knew it wouldn't abate.

So I lashed out blindly with
Floods and rains and earthquakes
That became a reality from myth
Causing a lot of unnecessary heartaches.

Now I live in stagnant pools
Collecting material memorabilia
Bottles and packets and other tools
They must be a part of my karma.

My abundance became my blight
Maybe because of my own doing
The constant depletion a horrible sight
The planet needs some urgent cleansing.

Hear me now or hear me then
The essence remains the same
The time will come only when
We stop this vicious blame game.

If I sound helpless, forgive me
I haven't been taught well
But help is where the heart will see
The tint of the Golden Bell.

So I ring my faithful companion
To help me find my flow again
It is a sincere call to action
For one of my fellow kinsmen.

THE SONG OF EARTH

I am the ground beneath your feet
I am the land, flat and serene
It is through me you really meet
The core, the essence, that has been.

I am the fourth Warrior now here
Bringing the past, present and future
Together as they unfold and appear
Each with its distinct flavour.

It's true I share a name with the Earth
My identity, however, is my own
Bigger than even the planet's girth
I stand firm, the dependable backbone.

From the time I was created
I have remained largely stable
To move even an inch I waited
For years on end in Time's cradle.

But once I was fragmented
Things started to change
Boundaries emerged and I lamented
This new definition felt very strange.

Visible and invisible lines criss-crossing
Across my clear surface
Leave me curiously aching
And a bit unhappy, I must confess.

If you think I am brooding
Down in the dumps, quite literally
Dark, heavy and constantly moping
I have been affected quite deeply.

As a Warrior you expect challenges
You march forth into the unknown
You cannot be the one who judges
You must remain as calm as stone.

But what happens when the unexpected
Attacks you from all sides
What happens when you are blinded
When on one of the world's biggest rides?

I was made to hold them forests
With roots that run deep
Tall mountains with sturdy crests
Stand alongside in a happy heap.

Endless meadows with fresh grass
Wet with early morning dew
The energy of which none can surpass
Even those with a celestial view.

The natural balance of things
Always giving in character
Suddenly met a clan of beings
That believed in the forever.

They looked, shook and took
Constantly worrying about themselves
Not realising that words in a book
Seldom remain inside shelves.

What I simply mean is this
What goes around comes around
The natural cycle do not dismiss
For the truth remains unshaken on my ground.

So if you wish to continue to choke
With plastics, waste and styrofoam
The consequences I can no more cloak
In the safety of my benevolent syndrome.

If you think you are freeing me up
From the flora, fauna and what not
With potted plants on terraces as back-up
Then your destiny (and mine) is fraught.

I do admire your sense of design
So full of precision and beauty
It shows you cannot confine
Man's natural creative ability.

But when did you stop to feel
The pulsating energy beneath?
Why did you deliberately seal
Your soul in an avaricious sheath?

I hear your call O Water
But I am unable to do
For I can't see the after
Of this catastrophic issue.

The earthquakes will happen
The landslides won't stop
The cracks will widen
The boundaries will flop.

Till there is such a time
That people see what we see
The atrocities of this crime
Will never set us free.

I call upon our collective wisdom
To find a solution together
To co-create our future's emblem
We need to meet in the Equal Chamber.

We can tide past this with caution
Of providence's multiple roads
Hope lies in the next generation
A magical time it forebodes.

EPILOGUE
THE FINAL SONG

The heavy sounds of anxiety
Echo around the empty Chamber
As the Warriors sit quietly
Looking for that elusive answer.

Equally helpless and angry
They fight their inner demons
Now isn't the time to say sorry
For unfortunate past actions.

There's no one to blame
Except the choices made
This wasn't some sadistic game
Where winners and losers fade.

They had been warned, they knew
By the One, so wise, so true
Who had with words so few
Given them an important overview.

The One would arrive any moment
And the Warriors were distraught
Each was like a nervous student
Wondering what such failure brought.

Would they be exiled to another planet?
Or would they be declared null and void?
They wondered what it would all beget
What if it were all destroyed?

They watched the door, waiting
Their attention now riveted
With apprehension quickly growing
They remained restlessly seated.

"Welcome, mighty Warriors
Why look so glum
You are meant to be healers
That's your innate wisdom."

The Warriors turned around in surprise
And saw the One smiling at them
In their minds it did arise
The One could from anywhere stem.

They quickly recounted their tale
And the One patiently listened
Weighing the options on the scale
With all that had already happened.

The Warriors waited as the One thought
About a possible solution to give
A counsel was now being sought
Hence, time to become pensive.

“Warriors, all journeys are a cycle
You must know when to stop
And start over from the anvil
Even if obstacles do crop.

“It is important to let go
And welcome the beginnings of change
Give it your best and do
Whatever be your range.

“Think what you would do
Instead of what they can
Put yourself in the other’s shoe
Answers will come in a wingspan.”

The Warriors bowed and left
And came back to the planet
They had to rise up and heft
This debris now, at the outset.

But it wasn’t something to do alone
They needed help by the hordes
Each one to his or her own
In charge of individual loads.

The Warrior's green guide will show
How every little gesture counts
The results might be slow
Though steadily it mounts.

The future is now in your hands
Take a hint and begin today
It's now your conscience that commands
It's up to you to obey.

The Warriors have taken the first step
And extended the olive branch
As the indisputable human rep
We hope at the challenge you don't blanch.

It's just one little thing a day
Of eco-living and awareness
Follow it for a year, we say
To help and decrease the mess.

This is after all our only home
We need to keep it healthy
If not nature's lengthy tome
Will pronounce the destruction decree.

We have the option to make it smooth
From one level to the next
This transition will only soothe
An evolution already indexed.

For wasn't it someone who just said
Every creation is a choice you bade
No one can rule your head
And that is how we are man…made.

GO GREEN!

One Eco-Action A Day
Keeps Global Warming At Bay

Eco-computing: A computer left on standby overnight uses enough energy to make thirty cups of tea. If you happen to spot one on at home, remember to switch it off.

Light Relief: Lights left on overnight use enough energy in a year to heat a home for almost five months. You could do your bit by doing the rounds, especially at night, and switching them off.

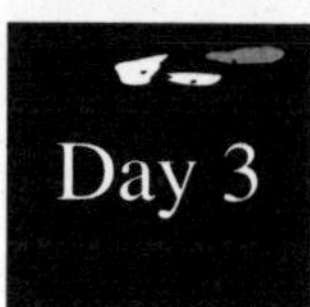

Utilising Leftovers: Throwing out leftovers not only wastes all the energy that went into producing that food, it also ends up in a landfill where it rots and produces methane, a potent greenhouse gas.

Tree of Life: Plant a sapling in your house or in your area or, better still, join a group that is trying to stop people from cutting down trees. Did you know that one bamboo tree is enough to provide oxygen for two people for a lifetime?

Leading Light: Suggest to your parents that the bulbs in your house be changed to CFLs (Compact Fluorescent Lamps). They use less electricity.

Baggy Ideas: Going shopping with your parents? Make sure that the bag that is carried along is made of cloth or jute. Do not accept plastic bags unless they are bio-degradable.

Recycle, Reuse...: Learn to ignore any product that says 'use and throw'. The motto should be: Recycle whatever you can. Start young!

A single tree absorbs one tonne of carbon dioxide over its lifetime. Shade provided by trees can also reduce your air-conditioning bill by 10 to 15%.

Dumping Garbage: Is the garbage in your house segregated daily? Ideally, it should be going into three containers: Plastics and glass in one, perishable waste in another, and paper waste in the third.

Throw a Green Party: Celebrating a special occasion? Opt for cutlery made of palm leaves and recycled material. If your birthday is over, you can suggest it the next time when a friend's birthday is coming up.

Not to be Brushed Aside: You might have heard this a million times, but do you actually do it? Save water by turning off the tap when you are brushing your teeth or washing.

Green Gadgets: Out of batteries? Opt for rechargeable batteries instead. Check out if this happens in your house.

Virtual Reality: Turn off equipment like televisions, DVD players, CD players, laptops, etc. when you are not using them. It can't be too much of an effort, for sure!

Green Trends: Send e-greeting cards instead of paper cards. Or better still, use recycled or one-sided paper to make your own card. Yes, people do appreciate the personalisation.

Planting Ideas: Do you water your garden? If you do, remember that it is best done either early in the morning or late in the evening. This reduces water loss due to evaporation.

Come Rain or Shine: Ask your parents if rainwater harvesting has been done in your house? If not, ask them to take steps to ensure that the work is undertaken as early as possible.

Waste No Time: Do you stay in an independent house, which has a backyard? If there is space to make a compost pit, it will turn organic waste into soil-enriching manure.

Charity Begins at Home: Give away your unwanted books, clothes, and toys to a charity shop. Do not hoard them; there are children out there who are not as fortunate as you are.

Pen Wise: Take a step back into the past and opt for eco-friendly fountain pens and bottled ink (not plastic cartridges), instead of plastic ballpoint pens.

To Foil or Not to Foil: Do you see your parents store excess food and other eatables in foil or plastic wrap? Suggest that ceramic containers may be used instead.

Fruity Facts: Make a promise that the next time you are in a fruit shop or a vegetable market, you will buy only those that are in season. This will help reduce enormous transport costs resulting from importing the items. And whenever possible, choose locally produced food.

V for Vegan: If you are a non-vegetarian, make this your Go Green Day and opt for vegetarian food instead. The consumption of livestock leads up to 18% of the world's greenhouse gases. If going veg is too hard a move, then make sure you at least avoid beef at all costs. Beef is the biggest contributor to greenhouse gases.

Crawling traffic contributes eight times as much air pollution as traffic moving at regular highway speed.

Paper Trail: Use one-sided paper to make little notebooks. Energy saved from a tonne of recycled paper saves enough electricity to power a three-bedroom house for an entire year. Pass on this information among your family and friends.

Bring to Light: Have you ever seen lit hoardings after midnight in your area? If so, ask your parents or grandparents and get them to talk to the shops and discourage the practice. They are a huge source of wasted energy.

Throwing your 'Waste' Around: Try not to litter the space around you, whether indoors or outdoors. Find the nearest dustbin or store the waste item in your bag till you do.

Cup of Joy: Ask your family members if plastic cups are used in their offices for water and beverages. Encourage them to use their own mugs and cut down on plastics.

Make up for Lost Time: Think before buying the next cosmetic product. Check if it has been tested on animals. You may be reluctant to switch to a new brand, but say no to animal-tested products.

That's a Wrap: While gift wrapping presents, use old newspapers or reuse gift wrappers.

Walk the Walk: As much as possible, walk where you can or cycle!

Green Signal: Have you ever checked if the ignition in your vehicle is switched off while waiting at a signal? It may mean a lag of a few seconds once the signal turns green, but definitely a practice to be enforced. Point it out, by all means.

Sign of the Times: Ask your parents if the sign boards and indicators in their work environment use LED (Light-Emitting Diode) lighting. LEDs can save up to 80% of the energy consumption for lighting.

Wall-to-Wall: How would you like to convert some walls in your home to "living walls" with vertical gardens? The idea of rooting plants in fibrous material and anchoring them to a wall was developed by Patrick Blanc, a Frenchman. Any takers for this idea?

Window Dressing: Take a close look at the windows in your home. Get your parents to replace any one clear glass with sun-ban reflective glass. This will reduce the power consumption in cooling.

A Just Cause: Here's something you can start out on immediately. Adopt any one environmental cause and see how you can spread the word locally.

Ship Shape: If your school is not too far away from home, start cycling to and fro. It not only reduces pollution but also helps you stay in shape.

In Harm's Way: Say no to helium balloons as they harm fish and animals.

The Three R's: Observe these three – Reuse, Recycle, Reduce.

Carbon Copy: Have you heard of carbon footprint? It is the amount of carbon released by an individual. Keep a tab on your carbon footprint. The question is not how big the party or occasion or wedding is but how small the carbon footprint it leaves behind.

Power Play: Ask your parents if they will consider switching to solar power at home, in whichever way possible, whether small or big. Every little counts!

Painting a Bleak Picture: Heard of any move to have your house painted? Tell your parents to consider, if it is really necessary. Decreasing the frequency of painting and paint removal contributes to a healthy planet.

Finishing Touch: Another step is to avoid the use of varnish and other coatings that are not essential.

Old is Gold: Take a leaf out of your grandparents' book and buy a mud pot for your house to store water in summer for naturally cool water, rather than use refrigerated water.

Nothing Ventured, Nothing Gained: Let today be 'Buy Nothing Day'. This sure sounds like an idea to be emulated, by the young and the old alike.

Paper Chase: Avoid taking printouts as much as possible as they use up energy, waste paper, and of course, result in empty toners and inkjet cartridges that are hard to dispose of.

Save the Day: Get everyone at home to reduce the amount of compact discs that are used and go digital instead by saving data in external hard drives.

Fly the Flag: Make sure you use as many organic things as possible during festivals. For instance, say no to plastic flags during Independence Day celebrations.

Idol in the Making: Use a clay Ganesha during Ganesh Chathurthi. You could also check out if natural paints have been used. Spread the message among family and friends.

Holi Hai: Use organic colours during Holi. Protect yourself from the health hazards of colours. So make a deal, and go organic this Holi.

A Breath of Fresh Air: Next time you see your parents pick up aerosol air fresheners while shopping, ask them to use incense instead. Aerosol has no practical reuse or recycling potential.

Wheels within Wheels: While driving, it is better to go slower with proper tyre inflation. It saves both fuel and the tyres besides lowering emissions. A tip worth conveying to elders behind the wheel.

Fuel Efficient: Check with your parents if a car pool can be arranged for your school and for them to get to work. See the difference.

Avoiding ten miles of driving every week would eliminate about five hundred pounds of carbon dioxide emissions a year.

Dry Run: Choose handkerchiefs and towels to dry your face and hands instead of tissues that are used and thrown.

Share and Share Alike: Do your parents buy many magazines and newspapers? Share them with friends or donate the used ones to hospitals, doctor's clinics, or community places.

Package Deal: Have you seen products made of styrofoam? Try not to use styrofoam packaging as it will never degrade. However, if it comes your way, reuse it.

Squeaky Clean: Did you know that with items like washing/ baking soda, borax, vinegar, salt, lemon, etc., you can do all your cleaning naturally and safely? There is no chemical involved.

Testing the Waters: Water-based paints are more air friendly than oil-based ones. An option is to look out for the 'Zero VOC' label. It is now available in India too.

Scrap Savers: About to toss away an aluminium can? Just a minute! Aluminium cans are unique because a can is recycled in sixty days. Making new aluminium cans from used cans takes 95% less energy.

Buzzword: It is said that a hundred thousand trees can be saved every Sunday if everyone recycled their newspapers. So, what's stopping you? Recycle the backlog of old newspapers and magazines in your house.

Parting Shot: Here's a snippet of information you can pass on. Look for electronic items that use recycled-content materials. For instance, IBM introduced a PC using 100% recycled plastic in all the plastic parts.

Chilling Facts: A tip for the busy beavers in the kitchen. Do not use running water to thaw frozen foods. Instead, defrost them overnight in the refrigerator, or by using the defrost setting on your microwave oven.

Down to Earth: Every day could accommodate the Earth Hour. Choose an hour anytime today and switch off all your lights to save the planet. Get your friends to do the same too.

Trump Card: Give earth-friendly gifts for birthdays or special occasions, be it cards made from recycled paper or a small potted plant.

Piece Together: Join Finland's Litter movement by picking up at least one piece of litter a day. A good way of leaving your carbon footprint!

All for a Cause: Is your family planning a vacation? As much as possible, support eco-hotels by booking into them.

Through the Looking Glass: Did you know that it takes a million years for glass to decompose? So, remember to recycle.

Strike a Match: Any idea if lighters are being used in your house? Promote use of matches instead of lighters. You can use cardboard matches, which are much more eco-friendly because they are made of recycled material.

Foodie Bytes: Do you like to dine out? Get your family to support local restaurants that use food derived from less than a hundred miles away, and learn more about the benefits of eating locally.

A twenty-foot side plantation inside a compound would protect the house from noise pollution of vehicular traffic.

Quick Fix: Get your parents to fix any leaky faucets in the house.

Shower to Shower: We should all be doing our bit to save water. Here's a great way to start. Try the five-minute shower – make it a goal for yourself.

Load Rage: Unnecessary loads increase fuel consumption. A reduction of weight by 50 kg can lead up to 2% saving in fuel, when driving in the city.

On a Power Trip: Ever heard your parents discuss ways of cutting costs? Plug your small appliances, TVs and clocks into smart power strips. When not in use, turn them off from the strip. This will save a lot of money on electric bills and is healthy for the environment.

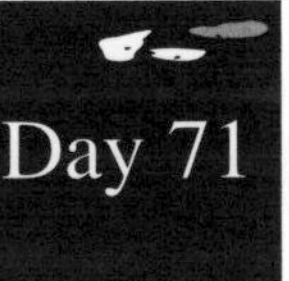

Clean Sweep: How can the efficiency of the refrigerator at home be maintained? Regularly cleaning the condenser coils found in the back or the bottom of the refrigerator will maximise its efficiency.

Message in a Bottle: Any idea what happens to the plastic bottles that we use? Ninety-five per cent of them are not recycled. Switching from bottled water to filtered tap water helps to go green and saves your money. Or suggest that your parents get a good quality water filter to make the tap water perfect.

On Everybody's Lips: Using plant-based oils, instead of petroleum-based chapsticks, really helps the environment and is more natural for the lips. Ask your mother, sisters and friends to give up petroleum-based lip balms for a greener alternative.

Green Sense: Outdoor lighting not only makes the electricity bill shoot up but is also disruptive to wildlife. Get motion sensors and let nature take back the night. It saves money, electricity and gives added security to your apartment.

Chew Over: Chewing gum is the second largest littering item in the world. Chewing gum is not bio-degradable and will stick to its surface for many, many years until treated. What about giving up that delectable item?

Sign of the Times: One simple way to reduce your carbon footprint is to sign up for e-statements, as it saves paper, trees, postage and delivery costs. Online banking, paying bills online, and saying no to postage or courier are good ways to reduce clutter. And good for the environment too.

Play it Cool: Is the window air- conditioner in your house kept out of direct sunlight? If that's not possible, consider building a wooden shelter to provide shade and help it run more efficiently.

It's Curtains: Are the carpets, rugs, window treatments and other textiles in your home made of natural fibres such as cotton or wool? Natural fibres are untreated and free of toxins, such as pesticides or chemical cleaners.

All Charged up: Don't charge electricals off a car battery. It might be convenient, but charging your iPod, mobile, laptop, etc. off the car battery greatly increases fuel consumption.

Pouring Oil on Troubled Waters: Did you know that every year each country puts about 350 million gallons of motor oil into the environment? It is possible that this oil can enter the ground and our water supply. Tell your parents to always take the motor oil to a gas station to have it recycled.

Wash and Wear: Wear clothes that don't need to be dry-cleaned. This saves money and cuts down on toxic chemical use. That sure can't be too difficult to follow.

Walk over: Once a day, avoid taking the lift and climb up to your apartment. It not only helps save the high power consumed by lifts but also helps you keep fit. Start young!

Cool as a Cucumber: Making sure that the drapes and shades are kept closed during the day in summer will prevent warming up the indoor atmosphere in summer.

Warm as Toast: Keeping the drapes closed at night will help keep out the extreme cold in the winter.

According to the World Health Organisation (WHO), within twenty five years, the present trend of global warming may cause the death of 3 lakh people every year.

Down the Drain: If used oils from vehicles are thrown in the drainage, it will mix up with water when it rains and result in water pollution. Spread the message to save water and never pollute the existing water.

In Full Flow: Did you know that a full freezer actually uses less energy than a half full freezer? Fill plastic jugs with water and place in the freezer to take up the extra space. Sound advice, indeed.

What's the Big Idea? Here's a green tip for the kitchen. Heating up a pan that is too large for the food being cooked is a waste of energy. Choose the smallest size pot or pan that will cook the food properly and save energy.

Behind Closed Doors: Opening the oven door during the baking cycle can lower the oven temperature by as much as fifty degrees. You can give baking foods a visual check through the glass portion of the oven door instead of opening it.

Money Matters: A washable, non-stick, reusable silicone mat can take the place of aluminum foil and parchment paper for many kitchen baking tasks. Anything reusable is a greener choice over disposables, plus will save money in the long run. Worth trying out.

Kitchen Culprits: Have you heard of phantom electric usage? Any electrical appliance plugged into an electric outlet is using electricity, even if the appliance is turned off. Tell your folks at home to unplug small kitchen appliances when not in use. The toaster, coffee maker and microwave are three big phantom energy users in the kitchen.

Letting off Steam: The steam that escapes from pots while cooking increases the cooking time and heats up the indoor air. So here's a tip for those at home. Place lids on pots, especially if they contain a boiling liquid, and the food will cook more quickly and use less energy. More energy is used in cooking and running the air-conditioner.

Sensible Shopping: Do errands in bulk. Make a list of the things you have to do, and see if you can fit a couple of those things together in one ride. That sure is doable, be it in your case or that of your family members!

Drop a Brick: It is estimated that flushing makes up thirty percent of a household's water use (about three to six gallons per flush). Placing a brick in the toilet tank will help conserve the amount of water used during each flush. Get your parents to try it out at home.

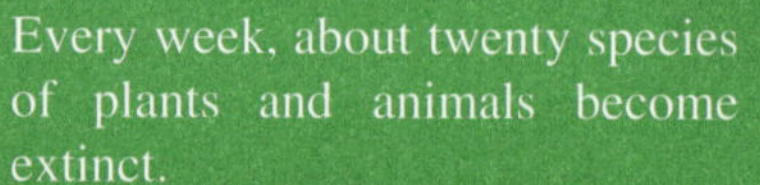

For the Couch Potato: Ever thought about how those chairs or sofas or throw pillows were made? Spread the message to seek out furniture and home accessories that are constructed from certified sustainable wood, reclaimed materials, bamboo, organic cotton and so on.

Lead the Pack: Pack your lunch in a reusable container and if you must use plastic bags, wash and reuse them for tomorrow's lunch.

Sunny Side up: Use the sun to clean and sanitise. Tell your parents to put cushions, sheets, rugs, clothes, and so forth out into the hot sun. To find out just how well this works, try putting a sweaty shirt in direct sunlight for a couple of hours. It'll smell like new.

Pot Them up: Do you have potted plants inside your house? Make sure that they are kept healthy. Healthy plants clean the air. Fake plants are dust magnets.

Dig up the Dirt: Check if the vacuum cleaner at home is battery operated. It's easy, lightweight, low-power, and can be used more often because it's less cumbersome. Do make sure that the vacuum cleaner bag is changed. Full bags leak like crazy and waste a lot of energy to boot.

Dirt Cheap: Air-conditioners too have filters that get clogged. They can be replaced inexpensively, or another option is to vacuum the dust and debris from the filter material.

Mood Swings: Did you know that the lamp is usually more influential than the type of light bulb in creating a mood? Lamps with dimmers are always good, and a lamp that focuses light lets you use a smaller light bulb and attain the same effect.

Heavy Metal: Avoid metal or heavy paper lampshades. Many of them cut off most of the light. Ask your parents to look for the ones that allow most of the light through. Diaphanous films are best.

Good, Bad and Ugly: Varying the intensity of lighting can create texture and depth in a room. If your parents are doing up the house, give them this tip. Disperse the lights around to highlight the good and ignore the not-so-good.

Cold Comfort: Vary wattage wherever possible. The higher the wattage, the colder the light. Bluish light “feels” colder than red. The lower the wattage, the redder the light, and the friendlier the tone. Decide what you would like your home or rooms to be and then go for it!

Small is Beautiful: A number of smaller light bulbs distributed around a room gives a soft colour and even lighting. Plus, lower-wattage bulbs have longer lifetimes because they're not being so stressed by heat. Isn't it better if some experimenting is done before plugging in what is on hand?

Zoning in: If your refrigerator allows different temperature settings for different zones, adjust the temperatures accordingly. Recommended temperatures are 37–40°F for the refrigerator, and 5°F for the freezer. Long-term freezer storage (deep freezers) should be set at 0°F. That's a useful tip, for sure.

No Icing on the Cake This: Defrost the freezer. Ice buildup makes for inefficiency. Chip in and do your bit to help.

One too Many: Eliminate overcrowding in the refrigerator. When the air inside a compartment can't move, the machinery has to work harder. Sure you'd have experienced this problem at some point.

Under Wraps: Is all the food in the refrigerator compartments covered? Uncovered foods release a lot of moisture and make the compressor work harder. Besides, if the food is not covered, it'll taste weird. Keep the refrigerator's doors closed as much as possible — an obvious piece of advice, perhaps, but worth stating anyway.

Self Help is the Best Help: Have you heard of self-cleaning ovens? These ovens are more efficient because they have higher insulation levels. What this means is that less heat is lost to the outside while cooking.

Auto Pilot: A gas oven with a pilotless ignition will help save 30% over its lifetime, and the air in your home will be cleaner. With pilot lights, some gas is always being burned (you can see the little blue flame wavering near the burner). With a pilotless gas stove, a spark plug type device ignites the gas when the burner is turned on.

Have your Cake and Eat it too: Convection ovens incorporate a small, high-temperature fan that moves the internal air in the oven compartment, thereby bringing more heat into contact with the food being baked. They are more efficient because baking takes less time, and less energy.

Raise a Toast: Small toaster ovens take much less energy than big conventional ovens. It is possible to get great browning effects if you know how to use them properly. Ask your parents to get one, if you don't have one already.

Dish Them Out: Did you know that it is possible to fill the oven with a number of dishes at the same time? This will lower the per-item cooking cost. If different items call for different temperatures, put the items that need higher temperatures on the top rack, and those that need lower temperatures on the lower one. That's easy to remember!

Rainforests are being cut down at the rate of a hundred acres per minute.

In a Dead Heat: Here's a tip for the cooking experts in the family. Don't preheat. Let the food warm up in the oven. And turn the stove off a few minutes before the allotted cooking time — the residual heat will finish the process.

Go with the Flow: If you've seen this practice at home, let on this bit of information. Don't lay foil on racks. Foil obstructs the natural flow of heat.

Pan Out: Food cooks more efficiently in the oven if glass or ceramic pans are used. The texture is better too. So the next time you buy a gift for your mother, you don't have to think twice.

Over the Edge: Match the pan to the size of the heating element. This way, no heat escapes around the edges. Time we started paying closer attention.

Keep the Lid on: Here's a surefire way to contain heat in the summer. Putting a lid on that boiling pot reduces the amount of heat and humidity that's released into the air. And remember to rinse pans out as soon as possible to cool them down.

Down the Drain: Now for a reverse tip. To release heat in cold weather, let hot pots and pans release their heat into your home. Don't rinse them out because that washes the heat right down the drain.

Behind Closed Doors: Beware, there are micro-organisms lurking out there! Leaving interior doors open whenever possible allows for better air circulation in your home. Even if that doesn't happen, you still benefit because closed-off rooms are much more prone to micro-organism breeding.

To the Four Winds: Whenever possible, open the windows in your house. Surprisingly, many people still don't think to open their windows. If there are multiple storeys, opening windows on different floors can increase the flow of breeze. Experiment to see what works best.

Door to Door: Add screen doors in the house wherever possible. Then the doors can be opened, just like windows. Enjoy the breath of fresh air.

Time Tested: Have you seen disposable diapers being used in your house? Try to stop the use. The number of diapers in landfills is truly amazing. Buy cloth diapers. They can be cleaned and reused. They have been in use for generations.

Throw in the Towel: Encourage the use of cloth towels instead of paper ones and durable plastic containers instead of plastic wrap, aluminium foil, or other disposable sealants. A lot of trash comes from meal preparation and storage.

Pack a Punch: Did you know that those little peanut-shaped packing pellets you find when you send a package last a million years in a landfill? They don't weigh much, so reuse them. Wonder who invented these things!

Paint the Town Red: If there are tins of paint remaining after the renovation at home, worry not. Mix them together and use the result to paint closets, garages, basements, barns, kids' rooms, and so forth. Paint is a real landfill nightmare, so why not use it up this way instead? Think of it as an adventure.

To a Tee: Seen your mother throw out old bath towels? Tell her to cut them up to clean the mess in the kitchen and elsewhere. They are good for cleaning tasks: polishing shoes, drying off pets, washing cars, and so on. You can do the same with old T-shirts too.

Every day, traffic jams waste thirty lakh litres of fuel worth Rs 11.5 crore.

Table Scraps: Here's how you can do your own composting. By composting the food you didn't eat, you eliminate the need for fertilisers and expensive soil treatments, and you save a lot of necessary landfill. Composters are available in the market and they make the job clean. Or you can compost in a hole in your backyard (provided you have one!).

Toning Down: Laser toner cartridges are full of resins and poisons, plus they take a lot of energy to manufacture. Tell your parents to insist on recharged cartridges. Old ones can be handed in at the same time. The Yellow Pages will list a store that sells recycled cartridges and takes in old ones.

Give and Take: Appliances can almost always be recycled. Drive your family to donate them when the new equipment is delivered (most appliance stores have active recycling programmes — they get some money for the old stuff, but add more power to them).

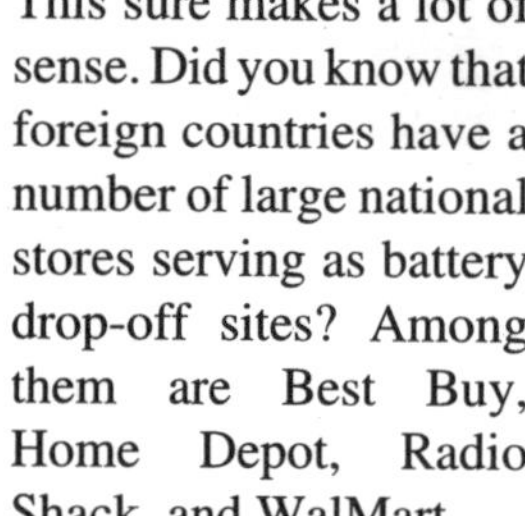

As Good as New: Old batteries can be recycled. This sure makes a lot of sense. Did you know that foreign countries have a number of large national stores serving as battery drop-off sites? Among them are Best Buy, Home Depot, Radio Shack, and WalMart.

Day 132

Go by the Book: You can recycle old books, especially the ones without any redeeming literary features.

Red Hot: Did you know that a furnace is the most expensive appliance in a house to run? In fact, household heating accounts for 60% of all energy used in the average home. So if you do happen to have one at home, make sure the filters are replaced every two months.

Blow Hot, Blow Cold: Ask your parents to install a programmable thermostat at home. Heating and cooling the house when no one is at home – or when everyone is in bed – uses an unnecessary amount of energy. This is bad for the environment and bad for the chequebook!

In Hot Water: If the hot water tank is getting old and there is a move to replace it, ask your parents to go in for one of the new tankless hot water options. They heat water as you need it instead of keeping an entire tank heated. As a result, they use significantly less energy, which is better for the environment. An added bonus is that about 50% can be saved on hot water heating costs.

Play it Cool: Closing the blinds and curtains and using ceiling fans can dramatically decrease the temperature of your home during the heat of the summer. If you must use air-conditioning, keep it at 75^{0}F and reserve its use only for the hottest days. Can there be anything better than keeping your house cool naturally?

Throw Light on: Make a move to replace incandescent light bulbs. Although they cost more upfront, the compact fluorescent light bulbs will save you a lot of money in the long run. They use 75% less electricity than incandescent light bulbs and last up to ten times longer!

Take on a New Light: A lot of people are guilty of leaving lights on all over the house. But remember that every little bit of electricity you can save counts! Make it a policy in your home to always turn the lights off when you leave a room.

Cold Truths: Did you know that refrigerators that are more than ten years old use approximately 60% more electricity than new models? To ensure that not more energy than needed is being used, keep the temperature of the fridge at 37^{0}F and the freezer at 0^{0}F. This will keep your food at the perfect temperature without using excess electricity.

Cold Comfort: A great tip is to clean the condenser of the refrigerator once or twice a year so that the motor does not have to run as long or as often. Are we so efficiency conscious? Give it some thought.

What's Cooking? Not all foods are great when cooked in the microwave, but there are times when it can be used over the conventional oven. Since the microwave uses 75% less energy than the oven, it's worth it to find new ways to use it when cooking!

It takes 60,00,000 trees to make one year's worth of tissue paper for the world.

Unplugged: Did you know that the television, DVD player, computer and kitchen appliances all use some electricity even when they are not turned on? Avoid wasting this electricity by unplugging the appliances if they are not going to be used for a day or longer. And remember to unplug them before you leave home for vacations.

Full Steam Ahead: When steaming vegetables or boiling water in the kettle, it is better to opt for countertop appliances instead of using the stove. They use significantly less electricity and get the job done faster. Very practical!

Full Cycle: Before running a cycle through the dishwasher, ask those at home to make sure it is full. Less electricity and less water will be used – and an added bonus is that the dishes will come out cleaner!

High and Dry: Letting the dishes air dry or using the cool dry option is better than the heat dry setting in the dishwasher. This alone will cut the amount of energy used for each load by 15% to 50%!

A Dimmer View: Having dimmers on lights is a great way to save energy, but some of the older styles are no more efficient than regular switches. Check if the switch feels warm. If it does, it's not energy saving. The new digital dimmers increase the amount of energy saved.

Warming up: Swimming pools account for as much as 60% of a home's summer energy costs – and more in places where pools are used year round. This can be cut down by as much as 20% by using a solar blanket to help keep the pool warm. Another 20% can be saved by turning down the pool heater by a few degrees.

Pipe Dream: Insulating the first metre of pipe leading into and out of hot-water tanks and any metal hot-water pipes running through unheated spaces at home will reduce the amount of electricity used and save some money. Have your parents tried this yet?

Clear the Dust: Having a full lint filter in the clothes dryer can result in 30% more energy being used. Be sure it is cleaned out before every use and scrubbed with a soft bristle brush every few months. Fill it with water and see if it drains. Tiny particles can clog the holes even though it appears to be clear. Is this being done at your house?

Set in Motion: Install motion detectors on outdoor lights. Instead of leaving on outdoor lights all evening, install motion detectors so they come on when needed. This relatively simple change can save as much as 30% of the electricity needed for outdoor lighting. A good idea to pick up. Do spread the message.

A tonne of recycled paper saves seventeen trees in paper production.

Out the Window: Ask your parents to ensure that doors and windows are sealed up. This will cut down on heat loss. In older homes, the attic in particular can benefit from increased insulation. It's well worth it to hire a professional to do an energy audit.

Slow and Steady: Have you heard of a slow cooker? Also known as "crock pots", slow cookers can be used for everything from roasts to stews. It is a cooking pot made of glazed ceramic or porcelain surrounded by a metal covering with an electric heating element, an energy efficient way of cooking.

Plugging Along: There are several places in a house where heat is lost. The electrical outlets are often overlooked, particularly in older houses where there is not much insulation in the walls. This can be prevented by putting in those little plastic child proofing plugs.

In Hot Water: Most houses have the hot water heater set much hotter than it needs to be. As a result, a lot of cold water is mixed in to get it to a useable temperature. Make sure the hot water heater is set to no higher than 140^0F. That is hot enough to kill germs but not so hot that it is a huge waste of energy.

Time for a Change: Changing the way we live is becoming so important that in many parts of the world the government and energy companies are helping homeowners by paying – or at least subsidizing – energy saving measures.

Waste Not, Want Not: A lot of utility companies now offer free energy audits to customers. It may be a surprise to know how much energy is being wasted in a house.

Buying Theory: When buying groceries, remember the four Ns. Choose food that is NATURAL (meaning no pesticides have been used), NAKED (as little packaging as possible), NUTRITIOUS and NOW (in season).

Day 158

Corner the Market: Most cities have farmer's markets where products can be bought from local vendors. Not only is local economy being supported but the items are also usually fresher and healthier. An added bonus is that the food wasn't trucked in, which means less fuel usage and fewer emissions.

Pack it in: The amount of packaging used for food nowadays is staggering. Help reduce it by opting for reusable containers. That sure is not a difficult task.

Strength in Numbers: Purchase oft used products in bulk. Buying in bulk helps cut down on the amount of packaging that needs to bc thrown out and less trips to the store to pick things up. Practical advice!

A Cut above: Composting your fruits and vegetables is an excellent way to cut down on the amount of garbage going into the landfill sites. It can provide nutrient rich soil that can be used in the garden.

What's the Catch? Running the tap while waiting for the water to heat up is a waste. Instead, catch it in a pitcher or pot and use it to water the plants. A sure saver, right?

Cutting Back: There are several things that can be done to cut back on the energy used when cooking. When boiling water put a lid on the pot and it will boil faster. Once it is boiling, turn down the heat.

Cook to a Turn: Most foods don't require the oven to be preheated so don't waste energy on this. When using the oven for cooking items such as roasts, you can turn it off for the last fifteen minutes and the heat left will finish the cooking.

Thaw out: It takes longer and uses more energy to cook foods from frozen. Instead, think ahead about the menu and thaw first. Likewise, take items out of the fridge before it is time to put them in the oven to bring them up to room temperature.

Bowled over: Next time a meal is being cooked, place a big bowl underneath the faucet and see how much water is collected while washing hands, rinsing food, etc. Reduce this wastage by keeping a bowl of water in the sink to wash your hands in. Keep another to wash fruits and vegetables in. This way only one bowl of water is being used instead of letting the tap run.

A Full Plate: Did you know there are paper plates that can be composted? The paper plates you are used to are made from virgin tree pulp. They are then coated in a petroleum-based wax, which means they cannot be recycled. But this new type is made from bagasse, a leftover from sugar processing. So now you can still be good to the environment and not have to do the dishes after a picnic!

Turn over a New Leaf: Plants are amazing at cleaning the environment. Having them in your house can reduce indoor air pollutants by more than half. Great choices are English ivy and peace lilies, which absorb toxic gases like benzene and formaldehyde.

Bitter Pill to Swallow: In almost everyone's medicine cabinet there will be expired medications. Do not flush them! That puts them into the water, which can be dangerous. Instead, inquire at your pharmacy about whether they will take them and dispose of them properly. If they cannot handle them they will at least be able to tell you where you can take them.

Adding Fuel to Fire: An open fireplace wastes up to 85% of the gas it uses because, like a wood-burning fireplace, the fire sucks heat from inside and sends it out through the chimney. Direct-vent gas fireplaces burn more efficiently and can save money.

Tub-Thumping: Use less water when you bathe. Baths typically use less water than showers. So whenever possible opt for a soak in the tub.

Our metros generate 21,275 tonnes of waste every day. 60% of the sewage goes untreated to our rivers and oceans.

Day 172

Short and Sweet: If you prefer showers, keep them short. Ten minutes is way too long. Ensure that a low-flow showerhead and faucet are installed to reduce the amount of water. Take this tip and cut back nearly 50% of the water used and barely even notice the difference.

Down the Toilet: Newer toilets use significantly less water than older ones. And the low-flush toilets not only conserve water but they actually reduce the greenhouse gases produced in the water-purification process. A great alternative to a new toilet is to place a plastic water bottle, with the cap on, in the tank. Doing so means less water is used for each flush.

At any Price: With the price of consumer goods getting less and less every year, it's tempting to simply replace old electronics and appliances when they break. But often they can be repaired for a fraction of the cost. Not only is money saved but that item is also kept out of the landfill.

High and Dry: The average household does more than four hundred loads of laundry in a year. That is a lot of electricity to dry all those clothes! This can be cut down dramatically by hanging your clothes to dry. In the cold months, opt for an indoor drying rack.

Take the Wraps off: Instead of wrapping paper, choose newspaper (the comics work great when they're in colour), reusable gift bags or even leftover wallpaper. Be sure to save up for later the reusable material in which a gift was packaged.

A Card up your Sleeve: Save your greeting cards and recycle them into gift tags. Why spend on something when you can recycle and reuse?

One Man's Trash is Another's Treasure: Have you ever looked at just how much waste your family generates in a one-week period? Next time you're about to throw something out, think of ways to reuse it. For example, old containers can be used for storage, stained clothing can be used as cleaning rags and broken hockey sticks make great garden stakes.

A Helping Hand: Instead of throwing out items you don't use anymore, give them to charity. Old clothing, shoes, home decor items, sporting goods and toys are all happily accepted by charities such as the Salvation Army. There will be less clutter in the garage and the donation will help families in need.

Off to a Flying Start: So much paper is wasted on sending junk mail and flyers. Put up a sign on the mailbox refusing these items and send a message to advertisers asking them to change their marketing techniques. If enough people do this they will eventually listen. Someone has to make a beginning.

Throw in the Towel: Using paper napkins and paper towels generates a lot of unnecessary waste. Do you know that the paper industry is the third greatest contributor to global warming emissions? A great source of rags is to use old clothes that are too stained or tattered to be worn anymore.

A Run for your Money: If yours is like most households, you will have a lot of things that run on batteries, everything from the TV remote to the camera. Do the environment a favour and use rechargeable batteries. They cost more upfront but they generate significantly less waste and in the end will save money.

Plastic bags and other plastic garbage thrown into the ocean kill as many as 10,00,000 sea creatures every year.

Throw on the Scrap Heap: A lot of people put out items week after week thinking they are being recycled when in fact they are being thrown in the garbage at the recycling facility. A way out is to stop buying products not sold in recyclable containers, besides ensuring that all of the garbage can be recycled.

On Dangerous Ground: Most municipalities have the means to properly dispose of hazardous materials such as old tyres, batteries, electronics, used oil materials and toxic substances such as paint and paint thinners. Ask your parents to check out if there is any move in your area to keep potentially dangerous materials out of landfills.

Count the Cost: Heating water accounts for approximately 15% of the average household energy bill, cut down by installing water saving showerheads and aerators on kitchen faucets. They use nearly 60% less water and chances are you won't even notice the difference (until you get your electricity bill!)

Clean as a Whistle: Did you know that almost all household cleaning can be done using vinegar, baking soda and water? Tell your family members that vinegar can be used as a natural disinfectant, deodoriser, all purpose cleaner and window cleaner. It can also be added to the rinse cycle of the laundry as a fabric softener.

Come Clean: Have the bathtub, toilet and counters cleaned with natural cleaning products, for example, a paste of baking soda and water. If your parents prefer to use commercial cleaners, get them to opt for the environmentally friendly versions that are now available.

Put it down on Paper: Many of the products used every day can be made from recycled materials. Seventy to ninety per cent of the energy is saved. In particular, paper products are a great way to choose more eco-friendly products. Look for bleach-free toilet paper and printing paper.

Choose Sides: A lot of the paper that is recycled has printing only on one side. Instead of using a fresh piece every time, print on the other side for documents that are not important. This paper can be reused as a scratch pad for notes or put together as a pad and kept next to the telephone for taking messages.

In the News: Daily newspapers generate a huge amount of waste. Even though they can be recycled, it is better to eliminate this unnecessary use of paper entirely. Ask your parents to read the news online instead of subscribing to newspaper services. Think about how much paper this will save over an entire year!

Every Trick in the Book: Libraries are a great resource for anyone looking to reduce the amount of waste they generate. Instead of purchasing books and magazines, check them out of the library.

More Harm than Good: The majority of dry cleaning chemicals are highly toxic. Not only are these chemicals harmful for the environment but they also remain on the clothes as you continue to wear them. This can present a health risk.

Come out in the Wash: When buying clothes, opt for items that can be washed at home. Keep in mind that most items that say 'dry clean only' can actually be washed by hand with a mild detergent and cold water. If the garment cannot be hand washed, look for a cleaning service that practises wet cleaning instead of dry cleaning.

A single quart of motor oil, if disposed of improperly, can contaminate up to 20,00,000 gallons of fresh water.

Deadly Warfare: Our society is obsessed with living germ free. And we may be hurting ourselves more than we're helping. Antibacterial cleaners contain a chemical known as triclosan, which is a form of dioxin. In addition to causing a variety of health-related problems including increased birth defects, it also mixes with the chlorine in the tap water and forms deadly chlorinated dioxins.

Soft Soap: We are better off just using regular soap. In fact, doing so will kill 99.4% of germs. Compare that with antibacterial soap that kills 99.6%.

Poster Child: Children are the future of our earth. If taught early, making environmentally friendly choices will become second nature to them. However, parents should also practise what they preach!

Well Disposed: The amount of chemicals used to create baby products today is staggering. Not to mention the amount of waste generated! Disposable diapers are the single largest type of garbage in the landfills. Spread the message and refuse to contribute to the problem.

Toy with the Idea: What about making the next Christmas 'battery free'? Tell family and friends to opt for gifts such as books, puzzles and non-electric toys instead of toys that require batteries to run. Make it a policy to only give battery-free gifts.

Foot the Bill: Almost all companies now offer the option of receiving bills electronically and paying them through online banking or telephone banking. Save all that unnecessary paper by using this service. Is this practice being followed in your house?

Cause célêbre: There are lots of different charities devoted to helping the environment. Whatever your choice, the important thing is to get involved. You'll feel great, help a worthwhile cause and be setting a good example for the other people in your community.

Tyred out: Watch your tyre pressure. Tests show that a 25% decrease in tyre pressure can cost you 5–10% more on fuel and 25% on tyre life.

Switch Back: Do you know that many companies abroad are now offering electricity that is generated from renewable resources such as wind and low-impact hydroelectric generation? If enough people make the switch, more and more companies will begin offering it.

Call it a Wash: Getting the car washed on the lawn serves a double duty—a clean car as well as a watered lawn at the same time. Plus a lot less water is being used than at commercial car washes. A bucket or a trigger hose attachment ensures that only the amount of water needed is used.

Day 204

A New Broom: Instead of spraying down pavements, patios and driveways with a hose and wasting water, get out the old fashioned broom. They're just going to get dirty again soon anyway!

For a Change: The best thing we can do for the environment is to make small changes in our everyday life. Add them all up and we can make a significant difference. Look at everything that is done in a day and see what can be done differently. For example, if your mother is a tea drinker ask her to only boil as much water as needed in the kettle.

One's Cup of Tea: Small reductions like bringing our own reusable mug instead of taking one of the throwaway paper cups can make a big difference if enough people do them.

Root of the Problem: Phosphates that find their way into our lakes and rivers are responsible for the overgrowth of algae. When this algae takes over a body of water, it chokes out the other plants growing on the bottom and causes a series of problems. Limit the amount of phosphates that end up in lakes and rivers by using detergents and soaps that are phosphate free.

Ring the Curtain Down: Polyvinyl Chloride or PVC is used to make many household items such as shower curtains, flooring and even toys. The entire process of making products from this material pollutes the environment—and they pollute the air in the house. Get people to opt for a cleaner environment and a healthier home.

Cheap and Cheerful: We have become a 'throw away society'. Instead of buying something because it is cheap, get your family to buy something that is good quality and is meant to last. It will cost more today, but the spending will be less in the long run as the product will not need to be replaced as frequently.

In Good Company: Companies that use recycled materials and package their items with less excess waste understand the importance of protecting the environment. Ask your family to buy such products to let the firms know that their eco-friendly mindset is appreciated.

Bag That: A plastic bag takes an estimated one thousand years to break down in the landfill. Think about how many are used with every visit to the grocery shop. That is a mind boggling amount of waste! Instead, use reusable shopping bags that are made of canvas. Alternatively, most stores have large cardboard boxes into which purchases can be packed. Spread the message.

Turning off the tap while brushing your teeth and soaping your hands can save around sixteen litres of water a day. That's 11,000 litres of water per person, per year.

On Second Thoughts: You may be amazed at the items some people are getting rid of. Next time your parents are looking for a product that may be available second hand, take time to look in the local paper or visit websites. Or instead, ask them to advertise for the item and have sellers make the contact.

Dressed to Kill: Even Hollywood has caught on to the vintage clothing craze! Next time you see anyone looking for a hot new outfit or the perfect necklace, ask them to consider a second hand store that has lots of stylish options from years gone by. The idea is to save those items from being wasted and look great while using it.

In Great Demand: In response to consumer demand, a lot of manufacturers are now making products that are organic or using all-natural materials such as bamboo. From clothing to hardwood flooring almost anything has been created in a more environmentally friendly way. It is worth paying a little more to help the planet.

Common Pool: Although it may take a little more organising to car pool, it can dramatically cut down on emissions. A city bus can hold as many passengers as forty cars! And the average seven person van emits almost seven times less pollution than a car with only one commuter.

Round the Trip: Studies show that the average person makes about two thousand car trips every year that are less than two miles from home. Instead of always using the car, try walking or cycling instead. Even if a portion of these trips can be converted, it would be cutting down significantly on the amount of carbon dioxide that is emitted into the atmosphere.

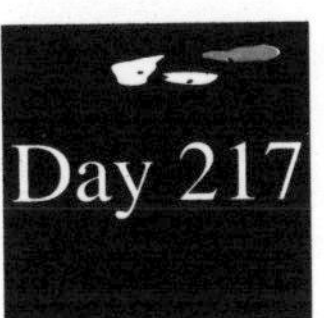

Take a New Turn: Not only does leaving the car idling waste fuel it also puts out a lot of unnecessary pollutants. A good rule of thumb is to turn the car off if you are sitting in traffic for more than ten seconds. Next time, make sure the person at the wheel does so.

A Head Start: Don't start the car ahead of time on a cold morning – the best way to heat it up is to start driving it. Making simple changes can save a lot of pollution.

Under Control: The most fuel is used up while accelerating. Not to mention the wear and tear on the engine and tyres, which makes the car run less efficiently. Save fuel—and cut down on emissions—by using cruise control when driving on the highway. Also, decreasing the driving speed by even a few miles an hour can save 10% on fuel.

Surface water in India is 75% polluted whereas it is 80% in China.

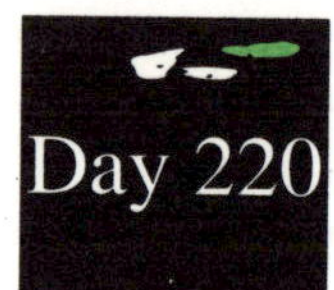

Oil the Wheels: A car that is in need of a tune-up or that has improperly inflated tyres will use more fuel than it needs to. Check with your parents to ensure that they are keeping up with a regular maintenance schedule to avoid any potential problems. This also includes regular oil changes and changing the air filter as recommended by the car manufacturer.

Acid Test: By requiring car manufacturers to make cars more efficient, the amount of carbon dioxide in the air can be significantly reduced. Ask elders to write to those in the government to raise fuel economy standards. Unless they are required to do so, car manufacturers have little incentive to do it on their own.

Asking Price: If your parents are looking for a new car, check out the options for hybrids. Although they cost more upfront, they will save money on gas and maintenance. But more importantly they can have a big impact on the amount of greenhouse gases that are released into the atmosphere. Or, at least look for the most fuel-efficient car available within their price range.

Thrift Trip: Instead of running out every time someone in the household thinks of something that is needed, plan ahead and make just one trip. Not only will less petrol be used but you'll also free up more time for things other than errands.

Day 224

Green Choice: Unfortunately, fertilisers never stay on the grass and flowerbeds where they are applied. Every time it rains the chemicals spread into the ground water, and end up polluting lakes, rivers and streams and even our drinking water. Spread the message to make a green choice by buying natural fertilisers. They cost a little more but are much gentler on the environment.

Day 225

Rain Check: Every time it rains, a lot of water goes right down the drain. Instead, ask your parents to have a rain barrel installed and capture this water for use on flowerbeds. A hose can be hooked up to most rain barrels and used to water the lawn.

Lead Kindly Light: A beautifully lit garden is a wonderful space to spend time during the warmer months. But make sure that solar or LED lights are installed. Solar lights have their battery charged by the sun all day so that they are ready to go in the evening. LED lights do use electricity but only a small fraction of what regular light bulbs use. In fact, one string of white LED fairy lights uses only two watts of electricity and the bulbs last up to a 100,000 hours.

Bitten by the Bug: Insects are a fact of life in the garden. And many are actually beneficial. But if they are munching on the plants, it's time to find natural solutions to deal with the pests. Instead of reaching for chemicals, opt for natural insecticides. For example, a saucer of beer will keep slugs off. There are also natural insecticidal soaps to 'wash' the plants with.

Breath of Fresh Air: Help make the air cleaner and the neighbourhood beautiful by planting trees in the yard. No matter the size of space you have, there is a tree that will work. Check with the local nursery about the spot where you would like to grow a tree and they will help select one that will grow to a manageable size and has a root system that will not interfere with anything.

A Bed of Roses: There are several things your family can do when preparing flowerbeds that will help you to conserve water in the garden. Make sure that native species are planted, because they are acclimatised to the amount of rain in the area. Also, ensure that compost is added to the soil to help it retain the moisture it gets.

Mix and Match: Large numbers of the same plants are much more likely to attract pests and diseases than a garden with a mixture. So make sure to mix it up! Not only will the plants be healthier but a greater variety of creatures can be attracted, thereby making for a much more interesting garden.

Knock on Wood: Although it is readily available and less expensive than other types of building materials, tell your parents never to use pressure treated wood when building fences, decks and sheds. It is full of chemicals that continue to be emitted into the atmosphere for many years. This is not only bad for the environment but is also bad for you as you breathe it.

Stand One's Ground: Peat moss is readily available at garden centres for use as an additive to soil. Its ability to hold moisture makes it very useful. And although having to water the garden less is great for the environment, peat moss is not. Peat is harvested from ancient wetlands and by removing it the natural filtration of groundwater is disturbed. A great alternative to better hold moisture in the soil is coir (coconut fibre).

A dripping tap can waste over 20,000 litres of water every year.

Grass Roots: By sowing grass that is ideally suited to the weather where you live, there will be less work to maintain it. Look for drought and disease resistant varieties at local garden centres and check out how to care for them.

Ready, Steady, Go: Drive steadily between 40–50 KMPH. Tests on Indian cars prove that you can get up to 40 per cent extra mileage at 40 KMPH against 80 KMPH.

Bet Money on: Did you know that some older lawn mowers actually produce more pollution than cars? Ask your parents to switch to battery powered or manual mowers. Save money and help the environment.

By Choice: When planting trees, consider the location you want to put them before deciding on the type of tree. This will ensure that you choose trees that will give you necessary shade when you need to stay cool and that will allow sun to shine in when you need heat.

Picture of Health: Create your own fertiliser by leaving grass clippings on the lawn. As they decompose, they put important nutrients back into the soil and make the lawn healthier and stronger. All those clippings are saved from going into a landfill site. Next time you see the gardener at work, ensure this practice is being followed.

Growing Pains: A lot of resources are needed to produce the food we buy at the supermarket. From the water used on the crops to the fuel needed for transportation, there are many negative environmental repercussions. Growing your own food is a great way to be more environmentally friendly. And homegrown vegetables always taste better! Why not try this out during the holidays?

Hose it Down: Choose an option that conserves as much water as possible while watering lawns or gardens. For small jobs, opt for a simple watering can. For larger jobs, choose a soaker hose. They use 70% less water than most types of sprinklers.

Every time we burn oil, coal and gas to generate electricity and power, we produce the heat trapping gases that cause global warming.

Fresh as a Daisy: Who wouldn't like to have fresh air while working? Ask your parents to keep a beautiful cactus near their workstation in the office to freshen the air as they work.

Cotton on: Planning to buy a new shower curtain? Purchase a cotton one to reduce the VOC or volatile organic compounds you breath in. Besides, it can be washed over and over.

A Head Start: What about starting an organic garden in school and creating compost for it? It's a large undertaking, but if you can get your science teacher behind you, it's likely that your principal will allow you to start an organic garden of some kind and a compost heap to fertilise it.

The Game's up: Playing video games on both computers and systems uses a LOT of energy! That's why your system or computer feels hot afterwards! You can save on energy by simply doing homework or going outside to play.

Breathe Easy: Get your mother to stop using Lysol or air fresheners of any kind. Think of how much of this indoor air pollution can be eliminated if natural air fresheners are used! There are some that can be mixed at home and others that can be bought. Either way, you'll be reducing allergens and toxins in the air.

Touch on the Raw: Eat more raw foods. Simply put, cooking less means less energy is being used. More vitamins and nutrients in the food will be retained. It's healthier for the family and the environment.

A Part to Play: Most children have more toys than they actually play with. Smaller children enjoy arts and crafts, and there are lots of fun and functional things that can be made from recyclables. This also means control over the paints that are being used, guaranteeing that there will be no lead.

Drawing the Line: Melt down crayon ends and make something cool out of them. This project is a lot of fun, and a great way to reuse something that would otherwise be tossed away.

Garden Variety: Plant a herb garden. It's good to have a reminder around where our food originates from. That sure sounds an interesting project!

True Colour: Instead of buying newer colouring books, ask your parents to bring back one-sided or unused paper from work and colour on the reverse side.

Stuffed Toy: Use your old pair of socks and convert it into an exciting toy for your friend. An opportunity to be at your creative best.

Green Challenge: When you go to the supermarket, do you ever check the label to see where your food comes from? If it says that it comes from your state or a state bordering yours, that's a great first step. But if you really want to make a difference, shop at a farmer's market, where you will find fresh, healthy and locally grown food.

Spare no Effort: Do your parents know somebody who deserves recognition for the efforts to take green to the mainstream? Start locally and get an organisation to sponsor a prize. Nominating your friend, teacher or a neighbour is a great way to show your appreciation. Good luck!

Take the Heat: Heating your home creates greenhouse gas emissions, whether your family uses electricity, home-heating oil, or a woodstove. In fact, heating and air–conditioning devours more than half of the energy that a home uses.

Create a Stir: Save money on a gift wrap that ordinarily gets ripped to shreds and thrown away. Make your own gift wrap by sprucing up paper grocery bags or recycled brown paper. Create nature stamps by coating leaves and flowers with non-toxic paint and stamping them on the paper.

Take the Wrap off: For gift wrapping that is reusable year after year, try wrapping your gifts Japanese style using a furoshiki. Furoshiki is a type of traditional Japanese wrapping cloth that was used to transport clothes, gifts or other goods.

Lighten up: Is there junk in the trunk of the car? Driving around with unnecessary weight makes the car less fuel efficient.

Slick Operator: Tell folks at home that the car uses less fuel when driven close to the speed limit. Avoid jerky starts and stops and use cruise control to maintain a steady speed. So, remember to ask them to slow down.

Road Sense: Ask your parents to get regular tune-ups and make sure the tyres of the car are properly inflated.

Put a Cap: Many cars have missing or broken gas caps, which cause gas to leak and harm the environment.

Don't Be a Drag: Remove bicycle and ski racks when not in use. Keep those windows closed when driving on the highway to reduce drag and improve fuel economy.

Route Around: Tell your parents to plan the route before setting out each day. This will help avoid sitting in heavy traffic.

Drop the Other Shoe: What do you do with all those old pairs of shoes? Believe it or not, even shoes are recyclable! There are shoe recycling centres abroad, where they are chopped up and made into new basketball courts, tracks, fields and playgrounds. Isn't it a great idea to drop those old sneakers off at such a centre? Who knows, you may find yourself running on top of them next year.

Burning and cutting millions of acres of trees each year is responsible for 20 – 25% of all carbon emissions.

Swap Notes: The toys at your friend's house always seem so much cooler, don't they? That's probably because they're new to you. One great way to get new toys and books and keep your mom from screaming is to have a toy and book swap. By having a swap, not only do you get to bring home all new stuff, you'll also help prevent pollution and save the energy and resources that are used to make toys.

Bark up the 'Right' Tree: The Earth is not just our home, it is home to millions of species of plants and animals. Help local wildlife feel at home by planting a tree that is native to your area.

At Every Turn: Turn off the lights when you leave a room. Close the blinds on a hot day if the sun is shining in. Dress lightly instead of turning on the airconditioning. Or use a fan.

All Walks of Life: Bike or walk short distances instead of asking for a ride in a car.

Hand in Hand: Take a hand towel to use instead of paper towels. Using the towel gives an opportunity to cut back on the amount of trash that paper towels produce.

A Grab Bag: Here's a way to raise awareness. Tell your classmates to bring in a reused grocery bag. For the entire day, they can drop their trash into it instead of throwing it in a trash can.

Look Good on Paper: Think up ways to cut back on the use of paper in the classroom and school. For example, use both sides of the paper, and spread the message to reduce the size of notices to fit on one sheet of paper.

Camp it up: One of the best ways to appreciate nature is to experience it. If your family cannot get away on a camping expedition, try pitching a tent in the backyard (if you have one). Spending the night outside, listening to tree frogs, owls and other night sounds is a great way to build memories.

On the House: Build a butterfly house, a bird house or a bat house. Better yet, build all three! Attracting birds and bats to your yard will help cut down on pests in a natural way.

Hold Good: Turn a cereal box into a magazine holder by cutting the sides on an angle and covering it with decorative paper, gift wrap or comics from the newspaper.

Recharge your Batteries: Suggest that your parents choose rechargeable batteries and then recycle them. The use of hundreds of single-use batteries equals the energy got out of one rechargeable battery.

Shed Light On: On the south side of your home plant a deciduous (leafy) tree that sheds its leaves. Its shade will cool your house in the summer. And when the leaves fall, sunlight will help warm the house in winter.

Cleanup Act: Participate in cleanup days at a beach or park. Use those outdoor trash cans! Never litter. Keep the waterways clean.

A Tangled Web: If you see someone killing a spider, tell the person not to. There are an estimated 40,000 species of spiders, and they all eat insects. They're an important part of the food web and provide natural pest control.

Kick up a Storm: Safeguard storm drains. Don't litter. Trash tossed carelessly outside often washes into storm drains, which empty into rivers and streams that eventually flow to the oceans. Pollution is a growing problem that has to be checked.

Last Ditch Effort: Don't ditch your pet. If you can't keep your pet, find it a new home, return it to the store where you bought it or give it to an animal shelter.

A Drop in the Bucket: If there is a dripping faucet in the house, ask your parents to replace the washer inside it. A faucet saved from leaking one drop each second, can save 2,700 gallons of water a year.

Have Enough on your Plate: Don't pile your plate. 'When's dinner?' you want to know. You're starving after a long day at school! Even so, restrain yourself and take only what you know you'll really be able to eat. Enough edible food to feed millions of people ends up in landfills.

Do the Dishes: Make sure that leftovers are scraped off the dishes instead of rinsing them. Wash the dishes soon after.

Make a Clean Sweep: Did you know that you can clean most of your house with a non-toxic cleaner? That magic bullet is baking soda. A little water and baking soda makes a terrific cleaning paste for tubs, sinks, stoves, and other surfaces.

On the Bright Side: Add a handful of baking soda to white clothes in the wash for brighter clothes. Baking soda is also a great deodoriser, and it won't irritate the lungs.

Think outside the Box: Opt for reusable boxes for lunches whenever possible. Throw-away bags and individually packaged lunch items are much more expensive than if reusable containers were filled up at home with juice, fruit and a sandwich. And that means less goes to the landfill too.

Old News is Good News: If any of you have a package to send, avoid the expense and waste of bubble wrap. Instead, reach for yesterday's newspaper as packing material. It might seem old fashioned, but what was good for grandma is still good for you.

Hand-Me-Downs: Organising a classroom clothing drive is easy. Ask each person to bring in one old but still clean and wearable piece of clothing that would otherwise be thrown away. The class can donate them as a group to someone in need.

Recycling one glass bottle saves enough energy to light a hundred watt bulb for four hours.

Coming up Roses: A memorable activity in which students can partake is planting a class garden. This requires a good amount of labour, as well as outdoor space and supplies, so it may require some extra planning. Class gardens can be an important part of a student's science education.

Open Book: Though they are fun and very important for a student's education, books can be harmful to the earth if they are not recycled properly. Rather than letting books get thrown out, students might be able to swap books in an organised manner if your teacher agrees to this activity.

Join Forces: Some classes prefer activities that don't require students to donate anything themselves. So fundraising for an environmental charity is one way that they can help the earth without putting an extra burden on their own families. If more classes want to join, a friendly competition can be hosted between classes to spur on the efforts.

Miss the Bus: Heard of a Walking Bus? It is a group of children who make their way to and from school on foot, supervised by two adults. Like a traditional bus, there is a fixed route with designated 'bus stops' and 'pick up times'. The idea originated in Australia in 1992 and has since picked up in many other countries. What a great idea!

Walk in the Park: Walk to a nearby park to examine the local ecosystems. There is no question of using extra petrol. You can rope in the children in the neighbourhood and make a great event of it.

Paint a Rosy Picture: Use water-based paints: The combination of these paints and a non-toxic creative project would be the ideal way to spend your holidays or evenings. Rope in your friends to do the same.

Pin down with a Label: Ask your parents to check the labels on the back of rugs just as you would on the back of any other product. Help the environment by looking for labels with natural fibres and green material. Most carpeting contains formaldehyde, but natural rugs and carpets can be made from recycled materials containing non-toxic dyes.

Burning Issue: Use a small burner which consumes 6–10% less gas than a big burner though it takes a little more time to complete cooking.

Zoning in: Have you heard of an idle-free school zone? These zones are catching on abroad and parents who arrive at school to pick up their kids are being encouraged to turn off their engines and reduce pollution. Isn't that a great idea?

As Good as New: Don't insist that you want new supplies when school starts every year. Use last year's supplies.

Make a Mark: Are you in the habit of buying bookmarks? Try making your own bookmarks and get your friends to do the same.

Not a Patch on: Reuse your backpack. Decorate it with cool patches and make it look as good as new.

Come in from the Cold: For those living in cold climes, put on a sweater or more clothes instead of turning up the heat in your home.

Energy-saving light bulbs last around ten times longer than ordinary light bulbs – over ten thousand hours.

Pin down with a Label: Don't use a screen saver. Screen savers are old technology, designed to keep phosphors from literally burning images into a monitor that has been left idle. That is why they involve patterns that jostle randomly across the display. They do actually use power, and can in some cases prevent your computer from going fully into power saving mode.

A Round Trip: Did you know that air travel produces large amounts of emissions? Therefore, reducing how much you fly, by even one or two trips a year can reduce emissions significantly.

Heavy Going: Avoid heavily packaged products. You can save 1,200 pounds of carbon dioxide if you cut down garbage by 10%.

Oranges and Lemons: Get those at home to use lemon juice as a cleaning agent. It bleaches, disinfects, deodorises, cuts through grease, and polishes brass and copper. Half a lemon as a scrubber, with baking soda for extra scouring power, results in glistening stainless steel sinks and aluminum pots.

Clean the Floor with: Stay clear of those ready to use disinfectants. Get your mother to use white vinegar instead. It deodorises and disinfects and can be used to wash floors, clean windows and remove stains. One part water to one part vinegar in a spray bottle is good for cleaning.

Water Table: Use optimum quantity of water for cooking. An experiment on cooking rice with double the required quantity of water has revealed that fuel consumption increased by 65% .

Wait it out: Get your family and friends to try the thirty-day rule. Wait thirty days after the first time you decide you want a product to really make your decision. This will eliminate impulse buying.

A laptop consumes five times less electricity than a desktop.

Up for Sale: Hold a second-hand sale. Children can learn the reuse message by taking any outgrown clothes and toys and selling them to others, rather than throwing them in the trash.

Animal Farm: Here is something for animal lovers. 'Adopt' an endangered animal through a charity. You could spread the message among friends and family too.

Babe in Arms: Is there a baby in the house? If so, tell your parents to make sure to get chemical-free bottles. Not only are they a good choice for your baby's health but they also help preserve the health of the planet.

Sweet and Simple: Here's how you can simplify your life. Keep only belongings that you use or enjoy on a regular basis. By making the effort to reduce what you own, you will naturally purchase less and create less waste in the future. Start young!

Need of the Hour: Ask your parents to buy used products whenever possible. If something is needed only temporarily, ask if a friend or neighbour would loan it.

Clean-up Act: Spend a day at the beach. Beach clean-up sessions will help children see the importance of properly disposing the waste. It's a perfect opportunity to enjoy the outdoors and learn together as a family.

Pillar of Support: When planning to stay at a hotel or motel, ask your parents to let the management know that you like to support businesses that adopt environmentally responsible practices, including reducing waste.

Up for Sale: Here is a great tip for your parents. A way to reuse products is to make it a point to shop at garage sales. Or better still, ask them to organise one with the help of family and friends.

Join Forces: Instead of investing in infrequently-used products such as lawn mowers, ladders, etc, ask your parents to join the neighbours in purchasing them.

Vegan Power: Switching to a vegetarian diet is a powerful way to help protect the environment and help ensure everyone has enough to eat.

Stretching your Money: By going green, your parents will save money. They can use this money to do have fun with the family.

In Harm's Way: Never release balloons outdoors. They frequently find their way to open water (even from hundreds of miles away) and can harm or kill turtles, whales, and other marine mammals.

Soft Soap: Check out environmentally friendly soap nuts to replace the laundry detergent. It can also be used as a general cleaning soap.

A Standing Offer: Offer or ask for gifts that don't involve buying anything. For example, when you have some free time together, offer to teach something you know how to do, donate to charity, plant seeds in your garden, or gift tickets to an event.

Green Thumb: The next time you have to give a gift, opt for something that keeps on growing. And what better gift than a tree! You could even ask for such gifts for your birthday.

A Mouth to Feed: Instead of asking for gifts during festivals and when planning to celebrate your birthday, suggest that your parents feed a child.

A Safety Net: Here's a fabulous idea for a gift. Give a mosquito net in order to save someone from malaria.

Watch the Clock: Have you heard of a clock that runs on water and a splash of lemon juice? Can't be anything but environmentally friendly, right! Ditch the batteries, as this clock runs for six to eight weeks of perfect timekeeping before it has to be refreshed.

A Good Egg: This is a gift that grows. Anyone with a window can have fresh herbs. All you have to do is to gently crack the top of the egg to water the soil after the seeds are embedded. Place it in the sun, and a miniature herb garden starts to grow!

Driving Home the Point: Draw a half a mile radius around your house on a map and ask your parents to only drive to stores in that radius when they are on their way to or coming back from somewhere farther away. Otherwise, walk.

Bombard with Questions: Question everything and ask adults to explain where things are made, and where they will end up. If they can't, ask them why not and then help them find out.

For the Record: Keep a record of everything you throw out for one entire week and then see if you can cut it in half the following week.

The Dark Side: If computers are being used for long hours at your parents' workplace, ask them to motivate employees to use a dark background to save energy. It looks cool and saves energy.

Bottling up: Make less use of plastic bottles for drinking water. Instead, fill water from home when going out. It is more hygienic and reduces landfills.

Do your Share: Don't buy movie videos and books. Hire videos and DVDs from a library. Download songs instead of buying audio CDs.

At least four hundred million people live in regions with severe water shortage. By the year 2050, it will be 4000 million.

A Raw Deal: Eat more raw vegetables which are healthier for you as well as save on cooking energy.

Garden Variety: Would you like to try your hand at gardening? Make use of empty milk containers to plant flowers, plants and vegetables.

Living Proof: Give your loved ones a living plant instead of cut flowers. The plant will stay green long after the flowers have wilted and been thrown into the trash.

In Good Condition: Instead of using a shampoo and a conditioner, you can opt for a two-in-one bottle. This will not only save a lot of chemicals and energy being used in the production of that extra bottle but also save landfill space when you have one less bottle to throw away.

Cool it: Is the food at your house cooled naturally to room temperature before being put into the fridge? Keeping hot food in a fridge uses a lot of energy while bringing it down to the right temperature.

Talk of Saving: Do your parents and siblings communicate through web video chat sites like Skype? This will save a lot of money and a billion gallons of petroleum for the world!

Doubling up: Using a dual SIM instead of two cell phones will dilute the burden on the Earth. Each cell phone is made of many metals and using dual SIM phones attracts less cost and minimum raw material.

Lip Service: Using plant-based oils instead of petroleum-based chapsticks will help the environment and is more natural for your lips. Ask those at home to give up petroleum-based lip balms for a greener alternative.

Make Room: Research has revealed that people living in one-person households are the biggest consumers of energy. It would be a good idea to get a roommate to share the house with.

Pull the Plug: When leaving the charger plugged in (not connected to the phone), it will still consume some energy. Do the rounds to see that this is not happening in your house.

Clear the Air: Are there any plants inside your house? Having plants inside the house will help filter the air and prevent attacks of allergy in those who are allergic to moulds, dust or synthetics.

Digging up Dirt: Have you seen dustbins that have a recycling mechanism? All the dirt and degradable stuff are recycled into useful stuff. It would be worth it to find out whether this is available in India.

Home Truths: Let us take a vow to observe Green Day at least once a fortnight. If only people would make the effort to follow at least a few of the green tips at home, office or the surrounding settings.

With every Breath: Humans inhale oxygen and exhale carbon dioxide. Green plants absorb carbon dioxide and give off oxygen. The more trees we have, the better we breathe.

Just 10% improvement in efficiency of water delivery for irrigation systems could conserve enough water to double the global amount available for drinking.

Smoke Signals: Have you come across soy candles? They are said to be free of petroleum, unlike conventional wax candles and are nearly soot-free. Therefore, they will not pollute the air in your apartment or leave those nasty smoke marks on your walls. They also burn up to 50% longer than wax candles.

The Root of the Matter: By watering less, grass can be made to grow roots that are deeper and healthier. Daily watering produces shallow roots. Do convey this information to the elders at home.

Be Fighting Fit: Tell your parents to start using tulsi plants. Keep one plant in your car. Putting tulsi leaves in drinking water helps fight various breathing disorders.

Bond with the Best: Have breakfast, lunch and dinner together to reduce reheating/cooking time. This saves fuel and you also invest in spending quality family time together. Remember to switch off the TV!

The Light of your Life: Solar lighting is a useful source of reusable energy, which, if used properly for common area alighting, will save a lot of energy. Automating the lighting system will further save energy. Do convey this information to family and friends.

Buckle up: On average, a lot of fuel is wasted by starting the engine and then putting on the seat belt. Does this happen in your case too? If so, it is time to mend your ways.

Don't Miss the Bus: Most airports have good public transport links, which means people can catch the bus or train instead of driving to the airport and adding to the carbon footprint. Make sure you pass on this information to friends.

In the Pipe: Take a look at the water connections in your home. One pipe can be used for water for drinking, bathing and utensil cleaning whereas another one can bring in rainwater and treated water for toilet, lawns, washing cars, floors, etc. This will save 40% of potable water.

Play it Cool: Make sure that all the air vents and the doors in unused rooms are closed in your house. By doing this, the heating and cooling systems will not have to work harder to regulate extra space that just goes unused anyway.

Under Pressure: Are pressure cookers being used in your house? If not, make sure the people at home know that it helps save the LPG consumed and the gas cylinder runs for a longer time. Besides, being a money saver, the nutrition in food is preserved too.

Work the Fat off: It has been found that fat and obese people produce one tonne of extra greenhouse gas per year. Maintain weight according to your body mass index. Apart from reducing greenhouse gases, it will keep you trim and in good health too.

Shot in the Dark: Refrain from making the room dark during the daytime and then using electric lamps. Instead, make full use of the sunlight. Electricity bills can be reduced to a great extent.

Soak to the Skin: For those who are into cooking remember to soak rice and lentils in water for some time before cooking. It not only helps save on cooking gas but is also good for health as the grains absorb water.

Save the Day: Do not use water more than you need. If your car is being washed at home, use a bucket and sponge. This helps in saving a good amount of water.

Fan out: Ceiling fans have a number of advantages over air-conditioners. The rate of carbon emission is comparatively less in ceiling fans than in an air-conditioner. The electricity consumed by an air-conditioner is much higher and the carbon released by it increases room temperature.

By 2025, population projections indicate that 75% of the world's population could reside in coastal areas.

Balance of Power: Personal computers consume more electricity than a laptop. This will save upto 90% of energy. Ask your parents to spread the word in their offices.

In Black and White: Is the exterior of your home painted in a light colour? Did you know that light colours reflect more heat than dark colours. For reflection of the sun's heat and light at window sills, light colours or white is a good choice.

Feeling Pressured: Pressure cooking saves fuel. Experiments have shown fuel savings of 20% on rice, 46% on soaked gram dal and 41.5% on meat as compared to ordinary cooking.

Be on the Line: The next time you plan to buy a paper phone book, think for a minute. Use an online directory instead. Try it out.

Down to Earth: On April 22, celebrate Earth Day by starting a new Earth-friendly habit. Spread the word! The more people treat the Earth well, the safer all its inhabitants will be.